J $11.95
363.73   Asimov, Isaac
As   What causes acid
rain?

DATE DUE

JY 29 '92			
OC 14 '92			
MR 29 '93			
JUL 08 97			
JUL 07 98			
AUG 01 98			
SEP 23 98			
JY 16 '10			

DEMCO

ASK ISAAC ASIMOV

WHAT CAUSES
ACID
RAIN?

BY ISAAC ASIMOV

Gareth Stevens Children's Books
MILWAUKEE

For a free color catalog describing Gareth Stevens' list of high-quality children's books, call 1-800-341-3569 (USA) or 1-800-461-9120 (Canada).

Library of Congress Cataloging-in-Publication Data

Asimov, Isaac, 1920-
    What causes acid rain? / by Isaac Asimov.
      p. cm. — (Ask Isaac Asimov)
    Includes bibliographical references and index.
    Summary: Discusses the nature and causes of acid rain, its harmful effects, and possible
ways to prevent it.
    ISBN 0-8368-0741-3
    1. Acid rain—Environmental aspects—Juvenile literature. 2. Air—Pollution—Juvenile
literature. [1. Acid rain. 2. Air—Pollution. 3. Pollution.] I. Title. II. Series: Asimov, Isaac,
1920- Ask Isaac Asimov.
TD195.44.A84 1991
363.73'86—dc20   91-50362

A Gareth Stevens Children's Books edition

Edited, designed, and produced by
Gareth Stevens Children's Books
1555 North RiverCenter Drive, Suite 201
Milwaukee, Wisconsin 53212, USA

Picture Credits
pp. 2-3, Kurt Carloni/Artisan, 1991; pp. 4-5, © Bruce Davidson/Survival Anglia; pp. 6-7, Kurt Carloni/ Artisan, 1991; pp. 8-9, © Gareth Stevens, Inc., 1991/Ken Novak; pp. 10-11, Kurt Carloni/Artisan, 1991; pp. 12-13, © Bill Bachman/NHPA; pp. 14-15, © RHPL/Picture Perfect USA ; pp. 16-17, © Phil Degginger/Picture Perfect USA; pp. 18-19, © 1992 Greg Vaughn; pp. 20-21, © Mark Edwards/Still Pictures; pp. 22-23, © L. Linkhart/Visuals Unlimited; p. 24, © L. Linkhart/Visuals Unlimited

Cover photograph, © Stephen Dalton/NHPA: A raindrop dripping off the tip of a leaf symbolizes the freshness and purity of rain. Unfortunately, in many parts of the world, the rain has become highly acidic. Acid rain kills many types of plants and animals.

Series editor: Elizabeth Kaplan
Series designer: Sabine Beaupré
Picture researcher: Diane Laska
Consulting editor: Matthew Groshek

Printed in MEXICO

1 2 3 4 5 6 7 8 9 98 97 96 95 94 93 92

Contents

Words that appear in the glossary are printed in **boldface** type the first time they occur in the text.

Exploring Our Environment

Look around you. You see forests, fields, lakes, and rivers. You see farms, factories, houses, and cities. All of these things make up our **environment**. Sometimes there are problems with the environment. For example, **acid rain** pollutes lakes and rivers and kills animals that live in them. It destroys forests and drives away the wildlife. What is acid rain? How does it differ from ordinary rain? Let's find out.

Rain, Falling on the Window Panes

Rain is water that falls from clouds in the sky. The Sun **evaporates** water from the oceans, lakes, and rivers. The water **vapor** rises and forms clouds high above us. Eventually the water in the clouds falls as rain.

There is only a certain amount of water on Earth. This water evaporates and falls as rain over and over again. The process that causes rain to form, fall, and evaporate is called the **water cycle**. The water cycle recycles the Earth's water in a natural way.

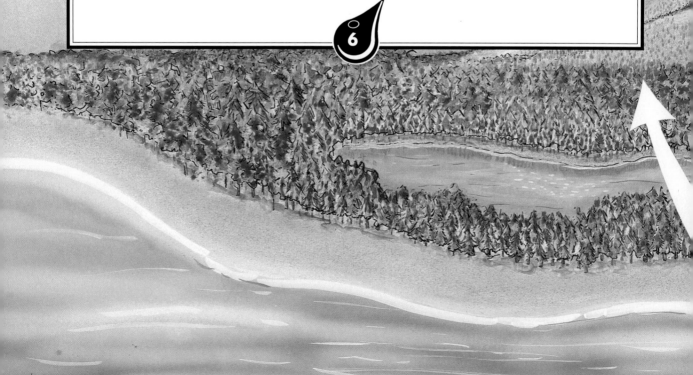

The Acid Test

Acids are sour liquids found in many living things. Lemons taste sour because they contain an acid. Spinach leaves and tomatoes also contain acids. There are even acids in your stomach.

Ordinary rain has only a tiny amount of acid in it. But acid rain is rain that has become polluted. This polluted rain can be as acidic as vinegar or lemon juice.

From Rain to Acid Rain

As rain falls to the ground, it mixes with gases in the **atmosphere**. Some of the gases contain the elements **sulfur** and **nitrogen**. When these gases mix with water, acids form. This is how rain water becomes acidic.

Long ago, acid rain wasn't a problem. Only in recent years has the rain become acidic. This is because the air is more polluted than it used to be. Air pollution causes acid rain.

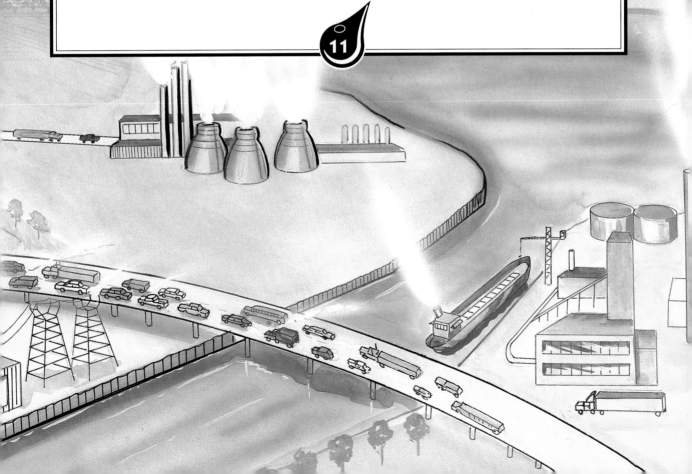

The Pollution Problem

In many places, you can see how polluted the air is. Look out over a big city on a hot summer day. You will probably see a layer of brown haze floating above the horizon. This mixture of smoke, dust, and gases is called **smog**. In some cities, smog hangs in the air for days at a time.

Burning too much coal, oil, and gasoline causes smog. The smoke from burning these fuels contains sulfur and nitrogen gases that cause acid rain.

Deadly Rainfall

Acid rain dissolves many types of rock. It discolors stone buildings. It eats away marble statues. It ruins structures that have stood for centuries.

Acid rain falls into lakes and rivers. The acidic water kills many fish. Frogs, worms, salamanders, and insects may also die.

Acid rain falls over forests and soaks down into the soil. Some trees cannot live in the acidic soil. Entire forests may be wiped out.

No Place Escapes

Acid rain falls all over the world. This is because winds scatter the gases that cause acid rain to all parts of the globe. So acid rain can form anywhere.

On the tops of mountains in New England, in the forests of eastern Canada, and in other places far from cities, towns, and factories, acid rain takes its toll. In fact, some of the world's most remote and beautiful places have problems with acid rain.

17

Who'll Stop the Rain?

The best way to stop acid rain is to stop polluting the air with sulfur and nitrogen gases that cause acid rain. Coal can be cleaned of sulfur before it is burned. The smoke that factories give off can also be cleaned. Devices called **scrubbers** remove sulfur gases from smoke.

Nitrogen gases are much harder to clean from the air. These gases form mainly in car and truck **exhaust**. Scientists are working on ways to cut down on these nitrogen gases.

What Can You Do?

Power plants and cars are the biggest sources of sulfur and nitrogen gases. So you can help prevent acid rain by using less electricity and by finding other ways to get around besides in a car. Turn off lights when you leave a room. Ask your parents to turn down the heat or air conditioning. Walk or bicycle instead of taking a ride.

Some trees take the acid out of acid rain. Planting and caring for these trees is another way to help solve the problem of acid rain.

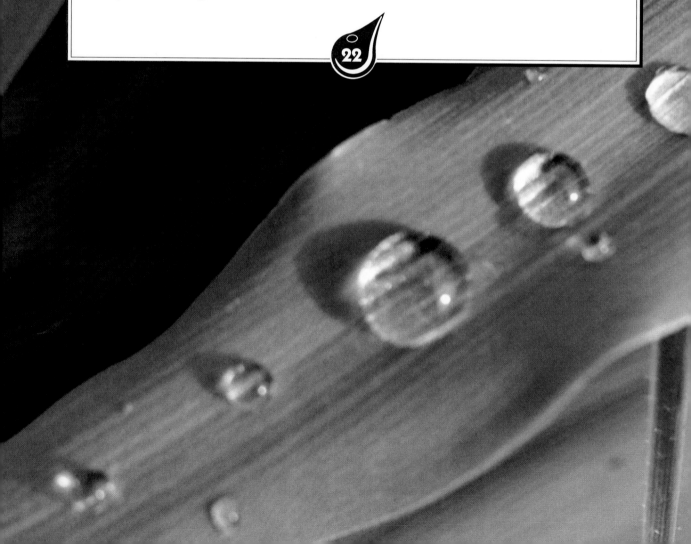

A Cleaner, Greener World

The problem of acid rain can't be solved overnight. It will take a long time to find clean sources of energy to replace coal, oil, and gasoline. But every little thing each person can do to reduce pollution will help. Look around you. Look for all the ways you can make your world a cleaner, greener place.

More Books to Read

Acid Rain by Katherine Gay (Watts)
The Acid Rain Hazard by Judith Woodburn (Gareth Stevens)
Acid Rain Reader (Acid Rain Foundation)
Acid Rain Science Projects by Edward Hessler and Harriett Stubbs
    (Acid Rain Foundation)

Places to Write

Here are some places you can write to for more information about acid rain. Be sure to tell them exactly what you want to know about. Give your full name and address so that they can write back to you.

National Acid Precipitation
    Assessment Program
722 Jackson Place NW
Washington, D.C.   20503

Environment Canada
Inquiry Center
351 St. Joseph Boulevard
Hull, Quebec   K1A 0H3

National Center of Atmospheric
    Research
Information and Education
    Outreach Program
P.O. Box 3000
Boulder, Colorado   80307-3000

Glossary

acid (ASS-id): a sour liquid; strong acids can burn the skin.

acid rain: rain that has become acidic by mixing with certain gases in the atmosphere.

atmosphere (AT-muh-sfear): the gases that surround the Earth.

environment (en-VIE-run-ment): the natural and artificial things that make up the Earth.

evaporate (ee-VAP-uh-rate): to change from a liquid to a gas.

exhaust (eks-AWST): the gases given off by cars, trucks, and other motor vehicles.

nitrogen (NIE-troe-juhn): a chemical element that, in its gaseous state, contributes to acid rain.

pollution (puh-LOO-shun): the addition of harmful dust, liquids, or gases to the environment.

scrubbers: devices that clean sulfur and other pollutants out of factory smoke before the smoke is released into the air.

smog: a type of air pollution that forms from a mixture of smoke, dust, and gases.

sulfur (SUHL-fer): a chemical element that, in its gaseous state, contributes to acid rain.

vapor (VAY-per): a gas that floats in the air.

water cycle: the process by which rain forms, falls, and evaporates on Earth.

Index